I0476217

First Printing: 2014

ISBN 978-1500826970

Lisa Harrison

POMO Creative

PO Box 4750

Sunshine Coast Mail Centre 4560

Australia

www.pomo.com.au

www.lisaharrison.com.au

Disclaimer:

While we make every effort to ensure that material in this book is accurate and up to date (unless denoted as archived material), such material does in no way constitute the provision of professional advice. Social Media Mastery does not guarantee, and accepts no legal liability whatsoever arising from or connected to, the accuracy, reliability, currency or completeness of any material contained in this book or any linked material. Users should seek appropriate independent professional advice prior to relying on, or entering into any commitment based on material published here. This material is purely published for reference purposes alone.

Dedication

My partner Stephen for believing in me and supporting me in creating Social Media Mastery over the last three years.

My two children whom I hope will be empowered and informed around the risks and benefits of using online tools as they grow from children to adults, the pressure of which our generation did not have to manage.

My sister Emma for your creative flair and giving me a gorgeous cover to take this baby out into the world.

Contents

Welcome

My Grandma's best and wisest advice to me was to work out what I love to do and then turn it into my job.

I love multimedia, the internet and building relationships and so I made a career out of social media, working as a consultant and helping others to use it, especially in their businesses. I don't just 'do' digital - I live and breathe it.

Let me tell you a little about myself. I'm passionate about digital media and using communications technology to connect people and I've been following my passion for over fourteen years now. I hold a degree with distinction in media and communications from the Queensland University of Technology. I've managed digital marketing programs for such organisations as the Royal National Association (RNA Brisbane Ekka), Birch Carrol, and Coyle Cinemas. In 2008 I became Director of Digital for leading Queensland creative agency, POMO with the aim of leading the company's strategic move into digital and social media marketing.

In 2012, I won the Professional Business Woman of the Year Award on the Sunshine Coast in Queensland and in 2013 I was a Queensland finalist in the Telstra Business Woman of the Year Awards. I spend time overseas every year attending cutting edge global think-tanks and conferences. In Australia, I'm a leading blogger, speaker, trainer and consultant on all things social media. But enough about me, what about the book you're holding right now?

It comes from one of my major career milestones which was creating the unique training course, *Social Media Mastery*. The course helps participants develop their marketing expertise using social media channels and leads to the nationally recognised Certificate IV in Business (BSB40212). I wanted to bring the contents of that course to a wider audience and this book is the result.

These days, all businesses need to master the use of social media. Most people are familiar with a few social media basics – LinkedIn, Facebook, etc. – but struggle with applying them to their business. You may have a Facebook page that is struggling to get off the ground, a Twitter account that never tweets, or you might be looking at tools like Pinterest, Instagram and Foursquare and wondering how to use them... With this book, I want to offer a business focus on using social media in all its forms and help you to leverage social media into direct and measurable business results.

I hope you enjoy reading it and I wish you good luck in all your social media marketing campaigns.

Lisa Harrison

Introduction

Getting the Most From This Book

This book will give you all the knowledge and confidence you need to use a variety of digital tools, from the planning phase right through to analysing and reporting on a digital campaign.

With the information in this book you will be able to:

- Write and implement a digital strategy to support your business aims and objectives.

- Rethink and integrate your traditional marketing.

- Understand the fundamentals of social media, e-commerce, websites, mobile applications, email, cloud computing, networking online and digital marketing.

- Use digital channels for customer service.

- Use key social media tools to network effectively.

- Develop and maintain business networks using social media.

- Establish and maintain business relationships using social media.

- Evaluate which online networking sites to join.

- Promote a crisp, clear representation of yourself or your business so others want to get to know you.

Although this is not a coursebook, the emphasis is very much on helping you to use the knowledge and techniques to create real and tangible business benefits. With that in mind, the contents are based on:

- **Global best practice** – incorporating concepts from a range of e-marketing commentators and leading practitioners, illustrated with examples from diverse industries.

- **Practical application** – giving practical insights into developing and executing plans and campaigns which can be applied in your business to improve campaign response rates. Throughout this book, I encourage you to take action in a planned and strategic manner.

What Lies Ahead…

You'll find the contents of this book are laid out in a straightforward and logical structure, as follows:

Chapter 1: *Understanding Social Media*

Social media offers a way to reach decision-makers, which might otherwise be very difficult to engage with using conventional advertising methods. In addition, this kind of networking brings with it the added advantages of recommendations, personal introductions, and 'word of mouth' for developing business opportunities.

Chapter 2: *Develop and Maintain Business Networks*

It is important that as a business person you are aware of the various digital strategies and channels that exist for developing and maintaining networks to profit your organisation, your team and yourself.

Chapter 3: *Establish and Maintain Business Relationships*

Relationship marketing hinges on the idea that new, non-developing, or transient relationships can be developed into long-lasting, deep and profitable ones.

Chapter 4: *Developing Social Media Strategies for Establishing Networks*

The goal is to think strategically about social media and understand how your business can approach the challenge, with clear aims and objectives.

CHAPTER 1
Understanding Social Media

Today's business owner faces not only the traditional demands – turning a profit, staving off competitors, maintaining employee satisfaction – but also a new challenge: **keeping up with the ever-changing world of social media.**

One might be forgiven for wondering, "who has time to figure out Twitter, Facebook and whatever the newest platform of the week is when there's a business to run?" After all, for those seated at the top, time is at a premium. Many employers and managers simply don't have enough time to delve into the world of social media marketing and understand how best to harness it for business success.

You need to understand what social media is and the advantages of using it for your business. When is it appropriate to use social media and when not? How will the social media landscape impact on your business in the future and how is using social media for networking an integral part of a successful business model?

What is Social Media?

More and more businesses are using social online networks to build relationships, meet new contacts to gain new leads, establish partnerships or broaden their audience reach, and all without ever having to meet a customer face to face.

Technology enables networking opportunities in ways that were not possible five years ago or even a couple of months ago, through online social networking sites such as Facebook, Twitter, YouTube, Instagram, Google+, etc. as well as blogging platforms such as Wordpress.

Social media platforms have a number of benefits for companies and are fast overtaking traditional media formats such as print and TV ads, brochures, flyers and email campaigns. On top of that, social media is now an integral part of your organic Search Engine Optimisation (SEO) efforts because of the links that social media can naturally generate to your website; using these links is now referred to as SMO or Social Media Optimisation.

But while the tools may be new, communication and interaction are as old as humanity itself. Consumers have always been "social" for they – as human beings – are social creatures, relying on others for vital information to survive and prosper.

We consult and listen to our peers, we pass information on to them. When we have something to offer, customers listen to us and then consult others and we do the same in turn when we are buyers. That's why so many essential principles of web communication haven't changed much from the old days of face-to-face sales and marketing.

However, what the Internet does change is the pace, scale, and cost of communication. You can send more messages to more people, more quickly and more cheaply than ever in history. Your basic message doesn't change just because you're using more efficient technology, but the language and the context need to be constructed appropriately for this new medium.

The best way to define **social media** is to break it down:

- "Media" is an instrument of communication, like a newspaper or a radio – one to many.

- "Social" is a characteristic of being human with a need for companionship, friendship and connection.

Therefore social media would be an instrument of communication for seeking or enjoying the companionship of others.

In **Web 2.0** terms, this is represented by a website that doesn't just give you information, but interacts with you while giving you that information. This interaction can be as simple as asking for your comments or letting you vote on an article, or it can be as complex as Flixster recommending movies to your network based on the ratings of other people with similar interests.

Think of regular media as a one-way street where you can read a newspaper or watch a report on television, but you have very limited scope to give your thoughts on the matter.

Social media, on the other hand, is a two-way street that gives you the ability to communicate in turn.

Understanding the Benefits Of Social Networking

With the Internet now integrated into nearly all aspects of everyday business life, many marketers and business owners are recognising the important role that social networking plays. Social networking will help your business gain contacts, clients, and can boost your public profile and reputation. Even entrepreneurs who run small businesses from their homes can take advantage of this resource to set up a truly global presence.

Social networking systems and online collaboration have become the **basis of electronic advertising for small businesses**. For example, Facebook alone allows business owners to communicate to the masses what they are doing, what events are taking place, and what achievements or recognitions have been received by the small business, etc. Relevant newspaper articles and other print media pertaining to your business can be scanned and uploaded to your profile or added to status or Twitter updates, allowing clients and potential clients to view your accomplishments within minutes of publication. Through this and other means, you can create a "buzz" about your business and your brand.

Whether on- or offline, the ultimate advantages of networking are growing sales, leads and forming strategic alliances. Yet social networking has many more advantages to help you grow your business. You just need to learn the right techniques. Social networking opens up new business opportunities all over the world. It can be daunting to dive into the virtual meet-and-greet world but don't be put off, the advantages are numerous:

- **Accessibility.** In many ways, social media levels the playing field for businesses as it is accessible to everyone, regardless of company size, turnover and contacts.

- **Range.** There is a wide range of social media sites (over 400 at last count) and tools you can use to be more interactive, communicating and exchanging information with customers. This number is growing every day.

- **Low Cost.** Social media tools offer more cost-effective ways to achieve your goals. Most sites are free with the main cost being time spent on updating profiles and interacting with contacts.

- **Marketing opportunities.** You can use social media to create and distribute content and promotional material, such as articles, videos and audio and all for a fraction of the money it would cost for this content to appear in the press, on the radio or on TV.

- **SEO.** Distributing content via social media provides you with more opportunities to entice others to visit and link to your website. This is a great way to enhance your organic SEO authority.

- **Research.** You can research your competition, customers, or partners.

- **Collaboration.** Easy connections with colleagues, customers, and industry thought leaders allow you to source feedback, test ideas and manage customer services quickly online in ways not available via traditional media.

- **Instant communication.** Through social media, you can communicate information instantly, regardless of geographical location. If a piece of content goes viral, there is no limit to the amount of people it could potentially reach, all at no extra cost to you.

- **Measurability.** With social media, you can test marketing messages and approaches, gauge user responses and tweak the message accordingly. This is done through the ever-growing number of free, easy-to-use social media measurement tools including Facebook insights and Google analytics.

- **Increased traffic and subscriber rates**. Having a database of subscribers to your newsletter or regular updates is a huge asset.

- **Word of mouth referrals.** The most valuable lead in business is that which has been reinforced through word of mouth from your loyal brand advocates.

- **Building relationships.** You can gain return customers and receive referrals by marketing the skills as well as services you offer via social networking.

- **Creating a profile.** You can benefit tremendously from a social networking profile that contains all the pertinent information that users need in order to evaluate your business. Your profile may include pictures of your team, products, completed projects, as well as logos and contact information.

- **Effortless messaging.** By targeting large audiences with a single click, messages and updates can be sent to all of your followers; just one of the many facets of social networking.

- **Opportunity to reward loyal customers by providing incentives.** You can provide contests, games, and prizes for clients who participate at a reasonably low cost.

Getting to Know Today's Social Media Landscape

Social media marketing is here to stay and, as mentioned in the previous section, the variety of options available to you (sites and tools) is huge and growing. However, you need to be aware that the more social networking options you utilise, the more time-consuming your strategy will be. The goal is to minimise the number of sites you use while maximising your reach. This means that as we all become more connected globally, there is a tendency for one site to dominate social networking worldwide.

Right now that site seems to be Facebook.

Besides Facebook, other popular social networking sites include Twitter, YouTube and Google+ with Pinterest rapidly increasing its share of users.

Whichever social media channels you choose to use as part of your strategy, you need to understand the underlying factors that are currently shaping the social media landscape. The following digital technology innovations will affect the way social media is used in the future:

- **Web 3.0 will mature into Web 4.0** – Tasks like your search for movies and food will be made faster and easier. Instead of multiple searches, you might type a complex sentence or two in your Web 3.0 browser, and the Web will do the rest. For example, you could type "I want to see a funny movie and then eat at a good Mexican restaurant. What are my options?" The Web 3.0 browser will analyse your response, search the Internet for all possible answers, and then organise the results for you. Web 4.0 will give us that pragmatic experience but combining Web 3.0 with mobile technology.

- **Employees will become an important part of companies' marketing teams** – Employees are the core to building a highly relevant audience of advocates for a brand. Make sure staff are familiar with your social media strategy and using the appropriate tools before engaging with the public. This way your staff will understand how social media tools and techniques can be effectively incorporated into your business.

- **Reputation management** – Your customer relationships will become increasingly focused on creating and managing perceptions. As social networks are used ever more frequently for aggregating and sharing interests, expect opinions (positive or negative) about products and services to spread with lightning speed.

- **The influencer will be even more influencing** – Each year, you will need to move the needle forward, scaling marketing efforts by creating and sharing information with employees and influential customer evangelists to help define your brand, products, and services from the ground up.

- **Social media return on investment (ROI) will be a top priority** – As you move from initial adoption of social media marketing toward the next stage of reflection and refinement, you'll be seeking data that clearly measures the cost-effectiveness of your social media campaigns.

- **Virtual teams will become more common** – The globalisation of the workforce will continue to mushroom with low-cost, easy access services becoming more prevalent.

- **(Geo) Location-based marketing will grow, and will be predominantly mobile** – Customer engagement and purchases will happen more frequently via mobile devices.

- **Facebook will advance social commerce and give Amazon a run for its money** – Facebook will provide an environment and online-shopping experience entirely different from the way we shop on Amazon.

- **Online communities will grow and take more power back from the corporate world** – Consumers possess a great deal of power through means of social media. The information they share becomes a trusted source and as a business you must engage, entertain and evolve to survive.

- **Video marketing will be the norm** – With Apple iPhone Facetime ready and Cisco predicting that 80% of all internet traffic will be video by 2015, we must embrace it in all its shapes and sizes.

- **Mobile apps will be an important part of engaging consumers** – The move towards mobile Internet has grown too large to ignore. 2014 has seen things accelerate even more on the mobile front. Customers have fallen in love with smartphones and tablets. Mobile search use is growing in leaps and bounds.

You Need a Social Media Manager (SMM)

With the progression, expansion and popularity of social networking sites, a new profession has been born: **Social Media Manager (SMM).** As the term suggests, the SMM handles the needs of your business when it comes to social media marketing strategies. Depending on the size of your operation, you might cover this role yourself, it might be a part of someone else's responsibilities, your business might appoint a full-time SMM from within the workforce, or you might outsource the role to a consultant or external supplier.

However it's done, the SMM role works in close coordination with your marketing and PR people and the primary responsibility is reputation management and the creation of inbound traffic.

This role requires a thorough knowledge of social media sites, tools and technologies. The SMM must know how to use them to communicate effectively, as well as create and maintain quality relationships with "friends" and "followers".

The SMM needs to make sure the company's presence on various social networking sites accords with an agreed social media strategy. Effective social media campaigns are conceived, launched and managed on a daily basis, ultimately creating a wider awareness of products and services. The SMM must likewise be up to date with current trends. With social media, you have to follow the trends or even better, become a trendsetter.

What's more, the SMM must always be ready to answer enquiries made using social media tools. One particular feature of social media marketing is that enquiries must be addressed rapidly. Social media encourages prospective customers to have short attention spans and if they are kept waiting, the delay may translate to the loss of a sale.

Part of the SMM role is to evaluate the effectiveness of the business's social media strategy. This involves producing comprehensive reports that gauge the effectiveness of all social media efforts campaigns.

Finally, it is essential that the SMM be a team player, collaborating with the marketing and PR teams so they can make successful campaigns.

END OF CHAPTER ACTIVITY – Your Social Media Usage So Far

1. Take time to think about what experiences you have had with social media (business or personal) and how it has impacted on your life (both positively and negatively)?

2. Now compare that with how you used social media two years ago. Acknowledge how much you have learned and how far you have come.

CHAPTER 2
Develop & Maintain Business Networks

Even before the Internet, social networking existed. In a nutshell, social networking is when a person uses already existing contacts to meet new people creating potential social or business links. Such links, in turn, will help expand future connections. Small and local businesses may already do this offline simply by attending community events or participating in trade shows, etc.

Anything that gets your company name out there, or connects you to helpful resources, is considered networking. Technology has brought this essential activity online, giving businesses the opportunity to further develop network relationships in new ways.

Social networking can be compared to the concept of the six degrees of separation, based on the idea that any two people can be connected through a chain of five or less intermediaries. Through social media sites, people join, and then invite their established contacts to do the same. Those contacts will likewise invite other individuals.

Today's approach to marketing, the approach that is infused with social media, leans heavily on the 4 Cs: Content, Context, Connection and Community.

Content + Context + Connection + Community = Social Media Marketing

Large quantities of relevant, education-based, and perhaps user-generated content is filtered, aggregated, and delivered in a context that makes it useful for people who are starving to make connections with people, products, and brands they can build a community around.

In order to fully leverage your social media networking opportunities, you need to:

- Use appropriate networking strategies to establish and maintain relationships that promote the development of business opportunities.

- Identify and pursue network opportunities to maximise a range of contacts.

- Communicate information regarding new networks to inform individuals, colleagues and clients of potential benefits.

- Participate in professional networks and associations to obtain and maintain personal knowledge and skills.

Laying the Foundations

Before leaping into some kind of social media or digital marketing activity (or anything to do with business for that matter) it is essential that you have a clear plan. Your social media marketing plan will consist of:

1. Aims and objectives

2. Ideal client identification

3. Available toolkit

4. Strategic Action Plan

5. Measurement/Assessment of results

6. Implementing a continuous improvement plan

Aims and Objectives – Be SMART

Use the SMART goal-setting approach to ensure your goals provide direction for you and your business.

S.M.A.R.T. represents the following:

Specific	State clearly what you want to achieve e.g. Increase my sales.
Measurable	You can tell when you achieve your goals when they're measurable e.g. Double my sales.
Achievable	The goal is within your capacity e.g. it is within your scope to do and you can reasonably expect to be successful.
Relevant	The goal is worth achieving within your planned time frame as it relates directly to improving some aspect of your business.

Specific	State clearly what you want to achieve e.g. Increase my sales.
Measurable	You can tell when you achieve your goals when they're measurable e.g. Double my sales.
Timeframed	Your goal is to be achieved by a specific date. Without a timeframe it will possibly be put off as other things arise e.g. Double my sales by the end of the Christmas after next.

Use your SMART goals as a touchstone for all your social media marketing activities and campaigns. Put simply, whatever action you are contemplating, ask yourself, "Does this take the business closer to achieving one or more of its goals?"

Ideal Client Identification

Ideal client/customer

Your success is going to hinge on how well you know and can talk to the needs and desires of your ideal customer. You need to know everything you can about that customer because it makes you a more effective communicator. Knowing your customer's wants and needs lets you talk directly to your target market segment and target your messages appropriately.

Types of social networking users

Forrester Research, Inc. is an independent research company that provides pragmatic and forward-thinking advice to global leaders in business and technology. Their program "Groundswell" helps organisations to understand and leverage the groundswell of technology and the social consumer, so that they can create a coherent social strategy. They describe the "social technographic" profiles of Internet users in terms of nine categories such as Joiners, Spectators, etc. For the purposes of classifying your ideal client or customer, I have simplified these, putting them into three categories of *Passionates*, *Influencers* and *Ad-Hocs*.

> **Passionates** – are people who care deeply about topics that are too niche to impact the mainstream zeitgeist. But within those areas of interest, they are acknowledged, respected, and taken seriously – even if their audiences are relatively small. These are often "the original bloggers" passionate about their chosen topic.

> **Influencers** – are people who have large groups of followers, across different online strata. They almost always started out as Passionates but have "crossed over" into a more mainstream role. Sometimes they are part of the modern media but this is actually fairly rare. The authority that an Influencer gained (while still a Passionate) has eclipsed traditional media's credibility.

> **Ad-Hocs (sometimes described as stalkers)** – are everyday folks. They deserve attention, too – though it is very hard to scale. By being patient and proactive with as many folks as possible, a brand marketer gains grass roots respect.

Determining Who Is Who

It's relatively simple, from a technological standpoint, to determine who is a Passionate, an Influencer or an Ad-Hoc.

First of all, 95% of the online population are Ad-Hocs. The Influencers, of course, are already well known. The Passionates are a little trickier to track down, it just takes time and manpower.

Influence measurement tools can help marketers to target the right people and manage online conversations. This is an ever-changing and evolving list but the current top tools are:

> **Klout** – Score-producing, public face that measures an individual's ability to move their networks to action.

> **Kred** - Kred is composed of two scores: Influence and Outreach.

> **TwitterGrader** – HubSpot's grader software were originally intended to be ego plays.

As to what you do with this information, how you engage with these three categories, from a process standpoint every case is different but typically you should follow 3-stage approach:

1. Pay attention to the Ad-Hocs immediately, universally and continuously;

2. Then, engage the Passionates make it easy for them to help you spread your message;

3. Finally, approach the Influencers, let them know you're there.

The Ad-Hocs should be buzzing about you in a nice way to give you the street cred to say hello to the Passionates — who are particularly wary of marketers. Win them over and you'll have advocates of your brand online, as well as a better-defined path to the Influencer communities.

This is a very simplified approach, but as a basic engagement strategy it holds up well.

Your Social Networking Toolkit

Types of social media tools

There is a wide range of social media sites that you can use to be more interactive, to communicate and exchange information with customers. This number is growing every day. Businesses are increasingly using these tools because they offer more cost-effective ways to achieve their goals.

With the vast number of tools, social media can seem like a maze. Does getting started in social media seem intimidating? Are you wondering where to find a qualified resource? Do you feel social networks and media sites are difficult, if not impossible, to track? You're not alone. Social networks were not primarily designed as marketing tools. So the rules that govern them are not always clear.

Social media is such a broad term; it covers a large range of websites. But the one common link between these websites is that you are able to interact with the website and interact with other visitors. Here are nine types of social media website:

- **Social Bookmarking** - (e.g. Del.icio.us, StumbleUpon) Interact by tagging websites and searching through websites bookmarked by other people.

- **Social News** - (Digg, Reddit) Interact by voting for articles and commenting on them.

- **Social Networking** - (Facebook, Google+) Interact by adding friends, commenting on profiles, joining groups and having discussions.

- **Social Photo Sharing** - (Instagram, Pinterest, Flickr) Interact by sharing images and commenting on user submissions.

- **Video Sharing -** (YouTube, Vine) Interact by sharing videos and commenting on user submissions.

- **Wikis -** (Wikipedia, Wikia) Interact by adding articles and editing existing articles.

- **Blogs -** (WordPress, Blogger) This is a type of website or part of a website. Blogs are usually maintained by an individual with regular entries of commentary, descriptions of events, or other material such as graphics or video.

- **Microblogging -** (Twitter) A broadcast medium in the form of blogging. A microblog differs from a traditional blog in that its content is typically smaller in both actual and aggregate file size.

- **Podcasts/Videocast -** (iTunes) A series of digital media files (either audio or video) that are released episodically and often downloaded through web syndication.

- **Geo-location -** (Facebook check-in, Foursquare) A service enabling you to share your physical location.

- **Music -** (Myspace, Spotify, Pandora) Playlists and radio stations you can share with friends or public.

The Three Parts of Social Networking

Some people use social media platforms as if they were all exactly the same. What they need to know is that each platform is different and should be approached in a completely unique way.

Facebook is a casual space (like a pub), LinkedIn is a space where you talk strictly business (trade show), Twitter is a noisy place where you share helpful links to position yourself as an expert (cocktail party), YouTube is packed with people clamouring for attention (Times Square on New Year's Eve) and MySpace… is pretty much history unless you're a musician.

When reviewing the different platforms, keep in mind that some of them help you to network (LinkedIn), others help you publish content (blogs), others help you to promote your brand (Facebook) and others help you to share content (Twitter and YouTube). Every social networking site involves the following activities:

PUBLISH - (journalist, author) Everyone can publish anything for everyone. Publish everything you have, anywhere you can, promote it, monitor what others publish, and empower your customers to publish.

SHARE - (public relations) Anyone can promote anything to everyone. Monitor what's being shared about you, find where your audience hangs out, promote your content and other content, produce content your audience will love.

NETWORK - (sales, marketing) Anyone can connect with everyone from anywhere. Make friends – find your existing connections, network through groups, add links to your email signature, blog articles, bio or profile…be helpful, answer questions, share interesting content and make connections.

Your Networking Strategic Plan

A networking strategy in the context of social media is a process of allocating limited resources to maximise sales and create a sustainable competitive advantage. In other words, a social media strategy is figuring out how to convert your limited amount of time and money into the largest business success. It's just as much about what you don't do as it is about what you do.

Before you consider any strategy, it is imperative you have a thorough understanding of your business plan as this allows you to pick your battles. It's a necessary part of the social media process. Otherwise, you'll spin your wheels on the unimportant tactics instead of going straight for the most effective solution.

In an ideal world, you'd have an infinite amount of time and money to devote to social media, and you'd reach your customer everywhere. But in the real world, you need a social media strategy.

Social Media Strategies

Sharing ideas & solving problems

More than ever, buyers are doing more of their own research online, actively seeking new problem-solving ideas and thought leaders for guidance and advice. To help buyers, savvy social media marketers are leveraging content that illuminates market trends, highlights issues others are successfully addressing, and provides tangible ideas on how to solve problems.

This strategy involves users actively listening to social media channels to maintain/gain and engage additional prospects or customers. This can include:

- Answering questions or queries about the company or products.

- Ensuring that campaigns are achieving the expected goals, driving the right responses, reactions and results.

- Gaining additional followers, connections and fans by tracking advocates and advocate reach.

- Monitoring for positive sentiment and use for promotion to gain additional followers.

- Monitoring for incidents/issues and negative sentiment to help mitigate these issues and limit risks.

- Monitoring mentions, requests or even competitors.

- Providing feedback to fine tune campaigns and content to meet user needs.

The more independent the content, the more credible it is. Similarly, the more timely the information, the more popular it is. Here are a few ideas on how to connect with early-stage buyers:

- Market opportunity research

- White papers

- Webinars

- Thought leadership videos

- Article highlights

- Thought-provoking blogs

- Interactive assessment tools

Spend some time using a listening tool like Feedly, Google Alerts or Social Mention to track conversations around brands or keywords. Use this information to find a solution to your target's problems. This could translate into an informational webinar or eBook.

Creating value

In the face of two economic downturns and the introduction of new technologies over the past decade, buyers have fundamentally and permanently changed. They seek solutions that can help them "do more with less," deliver fast payback, provide high ROI and realise superior value compared with other solutions.

Offering exclusive contests, discounts and deals are popular ways to connect with buyers who seek a "bargain" from every purchase. But price is not all that matters, so marketing can help economy-focused buyers discover the best solution by using social media to promote and deliver content that validates potential benefits, such as:

- Value proposition-focused white papers

- Webinars

- Success stories

Listen and personalise your engagement

Content marketing in the social domain isn't just about broadcasting, but about creating a collaborative dialogue with your followers, fans and connections. Here are the keys to personalisation success:

- Monitoring activity to determine who needs additional and personalised information and responses.

- Actively engaging the user base with follow-up responses, advice, posts and questions.

- Responding to and collaborating with participants on a timely, personal basis.

- Delivering competitive intelligence information proactively, yet credibly, to those seeking information about a particular solution or brand.

The marketers that appear most successful in generating engagement are leveraging the right content at the right time, and making the content more personal to create a dialogue with prospects to move the buying cycle forward, and engaging with existing customers to deepen relationships and drive loyalty.

Building credibility

With today's Internet-fuelled purchase decisions, trust must be gained through your digital profile as opposed to the traditional method of looking a salesperson in the eyes. Making a personal connection with followers, fans and connections is vital, and content with a personal feel (versus corporate veneer) tends to be the most popular.

Some examples include:

- Independent reviews

- Video testimonials

- Success stories and case studies

Entertain and Compel

Everyone needs a laugh now and then, and entertaining content is playing a larger role than ever in attracting attention and driving popularity. Entertaining yet thought-provoking videos, animations and cartoons are being used to great effect to gain followers, fans and connections.

The right content leveraged via social media channels is proven to drive more engagements and improve company popularity twice over those that fail to leverage content. Content aligned with the buying cycle and targeted towards ideas, value, credibility, personalisation and entertainment show the greatest success at driving engagement.

EXAMPLE – MERCEDES BENZ:

(https://www.facebook.com/MercedesBenz)

Consumers respond to the graphics and prettiness of well-crafted customised welcome tabs. We like offers, evidently (the stats seem to prove it). We like things that keep us in-system (within Facebook as opposed to sending us outside of Facebook). We like feeling that by being here, we're getting something special. We like sharing if it's something we like.

Campaigns and Contests

Campaigns involve coordinated communications to connect to and engage new prospects or existing customers via social media channels. Some campaign examples can include:

- Facebook fan contests to attract new fans.

- Timed tweets to promote a webinar.

- Research summary tweets to promote white paper.

- Syndication of a blog post to LinkedIn Groups to gain new connections and spur discussions.

Campaigns and contests drive interaction versus pure promotion, and they are more credible, often involving the voice of advocates, experts and/or third party validation.

The idea is to provide unique value to users, such as delivering special offers, exclusive events, or important content.

EXAMPLE – LORNA JANE

(https://www.facebook.com/lornajane.active?rf=111091648929850)

Lorna Jane is a leading Australian retailer of women's active wear. Lorna Jane aims to create products that will ignite enthusiasm for an active lifestyle. With a reasonably well-established following on Facebook, they decided to step it up and get their fans and customers to show the world how they used their products to 'move, nourish & believe'.

They created a Facebook competition that you entered by uploading a photo demonstrating how you 'move, nourish & believe' in order to win one of three Lorna Jane wardrobes valued at $500. There was no limit to the number of times you could enter and the premise was delightfully simple, as taking a photo and uploading it is second nature to most internet users and it reinforced the core brand message.

The Lorna Jane Facebook fan page received over 25,000 new Likes during the promotion timeline that ran for two months and created a 40%+ increase in visits to their promotion site. What's more, the competition entries provided valuable data capture that they could use to better understand their audience.

Collaboration

Collaboration involves creating and participating in a dialogue with prospects and customers. As opposed to the "push" target-oriented focus of traditional campaigns, collaboration is an interactive dialogue with followers, connections and fans for mutual benefit.

Collaborative innovation is all about engaging with prospects and customers via social media to provide interactive ideas, reviews, feedback and input around:

- Product improvements, termed "Social Sigma" by Forrester, such as market opportunity, features and benefits, design, pricing and more.

- Marketing improvements, such as slogan testing, campaign and promotional ideas.

- Business development, such as advice on go-to-market, channel or strategic partners.

- Advice, such as seeking and gathering opinion on operational improvements, and suppliers.

Choosing the right networking strategy

When you are choosing your networking strategy, you should consider your business strategy as well as the future of your business, your current resources and situation. You also need to consider the long-term potential of your strategy and how it may develop and change as your business grows.

Your strategy will change over time, but it is still important to ensure that you choose the right strategy for the present, in order to ensure that you achieve the success you need NOW before you can think about growth and expansion into new areas of the digital realm.

There are many different ways that you can cultivate beneficial business networks. Some strategies may yield immediate results while others may take longer to produce real benefits for your organisation.

Choosing the appropriate strategy for your purposes will become easier as you become a more experienced social networker.

Measuring the Results

The metrics you use to measure your strategy's success are a cornerstone of your social media marketing strategy. It's the only surefire way to see what works and what doesn't. After all, you don't want to spend $100,000 to buy a 30-second TV spot to launch your small business' product before you know it works. That's why digital marketing works so well because testing your marketing strategy on the web is easier than ever before.

Test, Measure, Optimise, Repeat

If you already have a website, you have your own market research platform. By altering your pages and studying changes in your web metrics, you can figure out whether the picture of your model looking left or right sells better, whether the glory shot of the watch sells more if it has a border or not, and whether more of your customers will subscribe to your newsletter if you put the subscription box in the top right.

Your website is the centre of your digital marketing universe, even if the website is your product. Every page needs to have a call to action (CTA) and actively market the action you want your visitor to take, whether it's to buy a product or to read the next article.

Considering the free Google Analytics tools (http://www.google.com/analytics/) and

Google Website Optimiser (www.google.com/websiteoptimizer) there is no reason you shouldn't be testing, measuring, and optimising every page on your site, NOW.

Continually Expand your networks

Most people network informally on a regular basis. You share information with friends, family and colleagues that you think is beneficial; for example, the name of a good handyman or hairdresser. By being aware of the many opportunities you have for networking, you can make better use of such occasions and expand your networks continually.

Every meeting is a networking opportunity.

Think about the opportunities you have for meeting people; for example:

- In the corridor

- At a staff meeting

- At social events

- Over coffee

- During a sales presentation

- At a function

Another way to expand your networks is to seek out new opportunities to network. Consider joining a special interest group or attending more functions. You could join a professional association or start subscribing to an email news group set up for members with interest similar to yours or via a social site such as LinkedIn. There are many ways to make contact with more people.

Make the most of in-person contact.

After you have made new contacts make sure you retain the information you have gained and contact them via the appropriate social networking sites. Keep an open mind about how each contact may be beneficial. Don't dismiss people because their interests are in a field unfamiliar to you. You never know when their expertise may come in handy. Some contacts may be valuable because they can put you in touch with others. They can be seen as a 'network partner' that you work in partnership with to establish networks.

Developing networking skills

Regardless of the strategy you choose, when pursuing networking opportunities you will require some key skills. The most effective networks are developed through excellent communication skills. Interpersonal skills are very important when building relationships with people. Some skills that you may need to practice include:

- Listening, interpreting and evaluating

- Making judgements

- Questioning

- Managing the information you gather and share

- Network by sharing

For ideas, tips and further research, try these options:

- The Marketing Association of Australia and New Zealand

    www.marketing.org.au – offers members a range of useful courses, publications and events to help build your business skills.

- Riley Guide

    www.rileyguide.com/nettips.html "Networking Tips and Pointers" are well summarised on this website.

- VentureBlog

    www.ventureblog.com/articles/indiv/2004/02/practical_netwo.php practical networking techniques are outlined here.

Finally, Beware the Bandwagon

The moral is that you'll waste your time if you try to market your business in every possible way. For every success story with a new media tactic there are a thousand failures because the businesses didn't look at their social media marketing plan strategically and pick their battles. When you hear about the latest marketing tactic or someone else's wildly successful marketing, don't assume you'll achieve identical results. You're better off going "deep" with a few tactics than you are "wide" with many tactics. And to go deep, you need to think strategically and test extensively. There is a low barrier to entry in almost all digital marketing channels, so dipping your foot in and testing the waters is inexpensive and easy.

END OF CHAPTER ACTIVITY – Effective Networking

If someone asks you, "What do you do?" how do you answer? Do you simply provide your name, job title and the company you work for? These days, that's simply not enough. To be blunt, it's not interesting enough to engage anyone. Creating an effective and memorable introduction and online profile means making sure all your social networking accounts have as much detail as possible.

What to do:

Build your FAB list. In other words, show the _F_eatures, _A_dvantages and _B_enefits of your products and/or services in a way that makes it easy for clients to decide to buy from you.

Here are some inspirational examples of big brands doing just that:

- **Johnson & Johnson** use their blog (http://www.blogjnj.com/) to show another side of the company, with frequent video posts and interviews.

- **McDonalds** maintains a blog to highlight the company's corporate social responsibility efforts.

- **National Geographic** uses Google's new virtual world, _Lively_, to bring people together around its show, LA Hard Hats.

- **Starbucks** started _MyStarbucksIdea_ so that customers can submit ideas for the company which are then voted on by other users; the best of which are implemented by the company.

- **Visa** launched _The Visa Business Network_ application on Facebook to connect small business users and to help them promote their businesses to a larger community.

END OF CHAPTER ACTIVITY – Identifying Your Ideal Customer

Using the diagram below make some notes on your idea client/customer. Be as specific as you can down to even giving them a name.

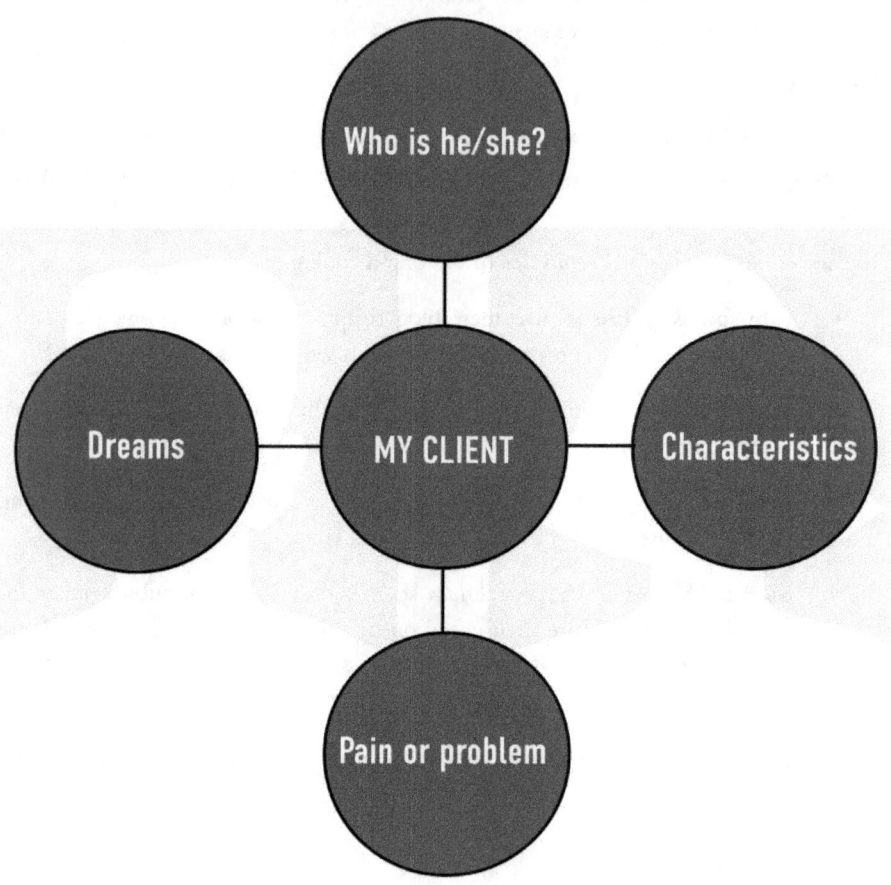

END OF CHAPTER ACTIVITY – Research Your Options

Within the types of social media tools you have a vast array of sites to choose from. Research one option that people in your industry are currently using to network. Investigate that option for uses, such as specialised groups, events or applications.

AN EXAMPLE

A **blog** is a website where entries or posts are listed in chronological order. Blogs commonly allow for readers to provide comments that are posted along with the original entry. For a better understanding of blogs, here are some resources:

Read these articles:

Wikipedia's entry on Blogs http://en.wikipedia.org/wiki/Blog

About.com's article "Anatomy of a Blog" http://webdesign.about.com/cs/weblogs/a/aa063003a.htm

About.com's article: "Frequently Asked Questions About Blogs" http://webdesign.about.com/cs/weblogs/a/aa060903a.htm

Blogging Basics http://www.blogbasics.com/index.php

Successful Blogging http://www.successfulblogging.com

Find and explore some blogs with these Directories and Blog Search Tools:

Technorati's Blog Directory http://technorati.com/blogs/directory/

Google's Blog Search http://blogsearch.google.com/

Blogarama http://www.blogarama.com/

Visit some of these Blogging platforms for creating blogs:

Blogger.com http://www.blogger.com/

WordPress.com http://wordpress.com/

Typepad.com http://www.typepad.com/

END OF CHAPTER ACTIVITY - Measurement

Start your digital/social media action plan or to-do list and consider the following questions:

- What are your digital marketing goals, how you will measure success? How can you set up your Google analytics with your website and social media accounts?

- Do you have adequate resources and budget to make your program as effective as possible?

- How will you plan for conversions (converting your conversations to leads)?

- How often are you going to assess the success of your digital marketing (so you can recalibrate, if necessary)?

CHAPTER 3
Establish and Maintain Business Relationships

The key to establishing and maintaining business relationships with social networks and contacts, is to follow through on the initial introduction or contact while there is still some momentum and enthusiasm from the meeting, however brief it may have been. Moreover, when you do follow through, aim to create an ongoing interaction that is genuinely of *mutual* benefit.

The key activities are:

- Building the trust and confidence of contacts through demonstrating high standards of business practices.

- Looking for benefits that are consistent with the requirements of both and the contact.

- Using a high level of negotiation skills to encourage positive outcomes.

- Identifying difficult situations and negotiating solutions using collaborative problem-solving techniques.

- Seeking specialist advice in the development of contacts where appropriate.

It is a fact that organisations that are committed to effective relationship management perform better financially while those with poor relationship management find it difficult to compete successfully.

Relationship-Building Strategies

There's more to business than just a transaction. Building a relationship helps you establish a bond. Some customers are even willing to pay more for a product and/or service if they have a personal connection with a company. From a PR perspective, building relationships is cost-effective because the only cost is your time. Here are some methods of investing in relationships:

1. **Touch base frequently.** If a customer recently placed an order or you provided a service, ask them for feedback. Showing you care about their satisfaction level speaks volumes about your commitment to them. It can also provide you with an opportunity to gain insight on other products and services that you can offer to gain new business. If they have not done business with you in a while, check to see how you can help them. It may

also serve as a reminder that they may need your product or service.

2. **Pick up the phone.** If most of your communication takes place via e-mail or via social media, it's still important to pick up the phone occasionally to touch base with your customers. Personal interaction is an important element in building a relationship.

3. **Branch out.** You may have a particular target market in mind, but to reach it doesn't mean that you network with just that group. Find groups that don't mirror your target market and build relationships with their members. That is the benefit of social networking: people you meet know people who might be future customers.

4. **Become a resource.** Stepping out to assist someone doesn't always mean you'll get an immediate return on your efforts. Refer a customer to them, help with an event or offer suggestions. When they, or someone they know, are looking for a product or service that you offer, you're more likely to be foremost in their mind. The more you get to know them, the more you'll be able to offer assistance by knowing their needs.

5. **Write a note.** Adding the personal touch of a thank you note to show customers your appreciation for their business is priceless. For the best impact, send it immediately after the event.

6. **Tailor your approach.** Your customers vary in workload, style of communication and desire to share information, so your approach should be just as diverse. If your customer doesn't appreciate unannounced visits, then call in advance to set up a time or invite him or her out for coffee. Remember your approach needs to be genuine and within their comfort zone or it may backfire on you.

7. **Be prompt with enquiries.** It shows your commitment to a high level of service and establishes confidence in you and your company. Also, if an issue arises, take action and make it your priority to resolve it immediately. Sometimes errors and how we resolve them provide an exceptional opportunity to show our commitment to the customer – take a bad situation and make it a positive.

8. **Listen, listen, listen.** Your customer may provide cues that are your gateway to providing a personal touch. If they indicate that their child is heading off to their first year of college, or they are taking a long awaited vacation, jot these things down on a calendar so you can ask how things went when you do a follow-up call. Or they might state that it was their birthday last week. Put that on your calendar so next year you can send a birthday greeting.

Developing your personal brand

To differentiate yourself from the crowded marketplace of social networking you'll need to create positive impressions on your clients and prospects through your personal branding. Your personal brand is your own unique and personal signature and the impression it makes on those you come into contact with, whether positive, negative or indifferent.

Step 1: Develop a persona and create profiles across the web - A great tip for getting started is to find and own one primary trait that makes you unique. For example, for Richard Branson, it is the idea of adventure. Adventure is part of nearly everything Branson does, from his websites to his social media presence. It is part of his signature brand. So if you can, think about something you can use to trademark yourself and incorporate that into each and every one of your online profiles.

Step 2: Engage with influencers about your topic - There are several types of influencers for every industry. When building your personal brand, the key point is that you should have a set of 10 to 20 influencers that you are targeting in order to extend the reach of your content and personal brand. You can identify your influencers by doing some online research (see the section in Chapter Two on just this topic), or by asking your prospects and customers who they rely on for advice and information. Once you have a list of influencers you are targeting, you can keep track of them using "interests" on Facebook, a customised CRM system, or even using lists on Twitter. Then, start engaging with your influencers by commenting on their content and sharing it through your social media profiles.

Step 3: Create compelling content around a certain topic - For content marketers, this tip should be a no-brainer: Remember to focus on your target audience's interests, issues, and needs in order to create interesting, engaging content that will be useful to them. When starting out, it makes sense to focus on a narrow set of topics and develop yourself as the thought leader in that space.

Step 4: Share your content to increase your brand's influence - Once you have created a body of content, be sure to share it in where those in need can find it. Naturally, this includes making sure to post it on your personal and company blogs. Don't limit yourself and your reach identifying opportunities to spread your influence outside of your immediate circle. Options for this can include:

- Guest blogging on an influencer's site.

- Contributing guest articles to a popular publication (online or print) within your space.

- Submitting yourself for speaking engagements.

- Attending meetings and events within your areas of interest/expertise.

If you do attend events, don't miss the opportunity to create additional content while you are on-site. Filming videos, posting session recaps, and offering to interview other participants are great ways to maximise your exposure at busy, crowded conferences and conventions, which can go a long way towards getting your brand persona into the industry limelight.

Managing Public Relations with Social Networking

Public Relations (PR) plays an important role in the digital revolution. That's because the mass migration of consumers to these new platforms creates both issues and opportunities.

At its core public relations is about maintaining reputations and those reputations are now being made online as digital communication becomes more accessible and mainstream. However, the rules are different in the digital environment as this new reputation economy creates an incentive to be more open, not less. In other words, being transparent is the key – simply putting out more PR spin won't work because people will either ignore it or even worse blacklist you. This brings with it many challenges and PR is at a point where it needs to re-evaluate itself within the digital communication technology domain.

This new battlefield is a smorgasbord of many different communication devices with no rules or conventions, few ethics and no geographic boundaries. Rumours abound and they can spread like a bushfire through the whole online community. It's often difficult to confront the perpetrators face-to-face and put forward a defence.

In this environment, the role of the PR practitioner becomes vital and managing online reputation is crucial.

There are three key social PR activities:

1. Responding to negative comments and feedback.

2. Resolving difficult situations.

3. Minimising risk through negotiation.

Responding to negative comments and feedback

The upside of social media sharing is that it creates viral, exponential reach. However, the downside is that negative conversations also reach further. Social media's transparency can be amazingly beneficial, until a less-than-flattering comment is posted, and then you face a decision about next steps. Responding can draw more attention to a comment. Like every other customer service interaction, you must carefully weigh the potential benefit or detriment to your unique business situation before proceeding with a response. If you decide to reply then response strategies for addressing negative comments include:

1. Acknowledge the comment, admit the issue and, where possible, explain how you're addressing it.

2. Where appropriate, erase the comment from Facebook. Be selective though, a well-managed criticism can be turned into a positive for your business followers – customers like to know complaints are handled with care and professionalism.

3. Monitor everything but respond case by case using a set of criteria that suit the nature of your business and the SMART goals of your social media strategy.

The third option is likely the most rational approach.

Resolving Difficult Situations

Think about the case of Greenpeace vs. Nestle. Think about Weinergate. Think about #Qantasluxury #McDStories. What do they have in common? They're examples of social media damaging business, and they're as abundant as Lady Gaga's Facebook followers.

Social media is something we should all embrace, but it's also one of the biggest risk management issues facing businesses today. So what do you do to stay ahead of the game? Well, with Facebook recently reaching over 1 billion users and a Twitter 'explosion' anticipated, ignoring it is no longer an option.

Developing effective business relationships involves interacting and working together with a range of people. In any work or personal situation involving groups of people there is the potential for differences to cause tension, which can lead to conflict. Sometimes people do not agree, they clash or misunderstand each other and problems occur.

That conflict can be:

- A clash of interest, values, actions, behaviours or aims.

- Real or imagined.

- Within a group or between individuals.

- Threatening to an individual, a group, their position, beliefs or goals.

Managing conflict and dealing with difficult situations is an important skill. However, difficult situations should not be seen as negative. If handled in an appropriate manner, they can lead you to a greater understanding of the issues at hand and help you find effective solutions.

Difficult situations are best resolved through a collaborative problem-solving technique such as:

- identifying sources of conflict

- identifying the problem

- analysing the problem

- developing options

- choosing options

- acting on the chosen options

EXAMPLE – FACEBOOK AND NESTLÉ

Thanks to Facebook and other social media channels, the Nestlé Company had an enormous public relations mess on their hands in 2010. The environmental protection group Greenpeace, who are known for their unorthodox and sometimes heavy-handed ways of bringing attention to issues, created a parody video (but it's somewhat gory, not funny) on YouTube of Nestlé's Kit Kat candy bar product. The video suggests that the production of a key ingredient, palm oil, helps further the destruction of rainforests, which in turn threatens endangered species such as the Orangutan. Greenpeace says that the Paradise Forests in Sumatra in particular are suffering a record-breaking deforestation rate.

Nestlé reacted by requesting that YouTube take it down. Viewer comments suggest that it was taken down, but that did not stop the video from reappearing on multiple video-sharing sites, in multiple copies.

In addition to the Greenpeace video, there was an animated parody of Nestlé's reaction. In it, two animated characters (using xtranormal.com's web software) pretend to be Nestlé employees and talk about how they'll get the Greenpeace video removed by citing copyright violation.

Consumers then attacked Nestlé on their Facebook Page. The 140+-year-old Swiss-based company's page soon had over 93,000 fans, and some may have been legit, but many people joined just to voice their opposition, reminding people of past Nestlé controversies, namely their breast milk substitutes.

Nestle then fired the heavy artillery at everyone, fans and activists alike, which did far more damage than anything Greenpeace could say, creating further opposition. As one fan wrote on the Nestlé Facebook page:

"I was a big fan of your products, but now, when I saw what you guys wrote, I think I'm gonna stop buying them."

With an increasing number of companies using social media, especially Facebook fan pages, to interact with consumers, it's important to get it right. There's an obvious lesson here for companies: if you do something wrong and people attack you through social media, being defensive gets you nowhere. There might be a lot of apathy about many important worldwide concerns, including the environment, but social media makes it easy for those who like to be vocal to actually be vocal and instigate concern. Once grassroots concern goes viral, social media can turn anti-social as far as your business is concerned.

Minimising Risk Through Negotiation

Another social media PR activity is to minimise the risk of damage to the company's reputation by negotiation. This process involves a number of steps:

- Actively engage on social network venues to understand how reputation can be impacted by the interactions.

- Gather information on the social media activities your company is considering. Then assess the areas of vulnerability, create counteraction plans and communicate them to employees.

- Develop a comprehensive "new media" policy. The policy should establish the ground rules for all employees — not just those in marketing — on communicating online, including social networking.

- Establish a social media point person (the SMM or Social Media Manager). There should be at least one person, if not a team, in charge of overseeing the company's social media activities and responding in the event of a crisis.

- Review every country's laws and regulations related to social media. Even within the European Union, laws can be implemented differently. Don't take legal or regulatory compliance for granted.

- Review insurance policies to see whether they provide coverage for risks arising from social media. General liability policies have very restrictive coverage regarding advertising injuries. Even so, there may be coverage under a number of policies, including directors and officers, errors and omissions, property, fidelity bond, fiduciary liability, as well as general liability. Cyber liability policies also may respond in certain cases.

Seek Advice On How To Develop Contacts

Establishing and maintaining contact with your network can require work and a specific set of skills. Some people find it difficult to make new contacts or keep in touch with those they have. This might be because of time constraints or they may feel they lack those communication, personal or technical skills to develop an effective business relationship. Spend some time developing your expertise in person which will ultimately contribute to your online networks.

It is often a good idea to speak to experienced people, such as your manager or a mentor, to identify how they manage this important aspect of their work. For example ask questions like "I am not sure how to advance the relationship once it is established, so how can I demonstrate that they can trust me?" And "What can I do to maximise the benefits to our organisation?"

Watch others in action. Follow those who you admire and see how they use their expertise to approach and develop a contact's confidence and trust.

Finally, Treat People With Respect, Empathy And Integrity

When establishing and maintaining your online business relationships, given the distant nature of the communication, it is more important than ever to bear in mind that good relationships are founded on respect, empathy and integrity.

- Treating people with respect means listening to what they have to say, trying not to prejudge them and respecting their opinions, even if you do not agree with them. When online you also need to understand that the context in which the person is reading or writing is going is be very different from your perception.

- Show respect by remaining polite and treating people courteously, even if they are behaving unreasonably. Avoid reacting emotionally.

- Empathy refers to listening to others and showing that you understand their situation. You do not have to sympathise or agree with them; instead try to understand what they are thinking and feeling – place yourself in their shoes. By showing genuine interest in people, you will soon be on the path to developing trust, rapport and a positive relationship.

Remember that in all your business transactions you must behave appropriately, according to your organisation's standards for privacy, confidentiality and security.

END OF CHAPTER ACTIVITY- Building a relationship

Building any type of a relationship takes time, whether it's a personal or business relationship. It's an essential part of your business to help maintain and grow your customer base. As part of your daily to-do list, make a point to touch one customer every day. You may be surprised at the impact.

END OF CHAPTER ACTIVITY – Personal Branding

If you haven't already developed yours on Twitter, Facebook, LinkedIn, Google+, Pinterest and About.me, get started today. Start with one social tool you're comfortable with before moving onto another. You may even consider setting up your own website or personal blog.

CHAPTER 4
Developing Social Media Strategies
for Establishing Networks

With more companies flocking to Web 2.0 to gain exposure, there is a Catch-22 situation faced by most organisations looking to leverage social networking. On the one hand, taking an honest, natural and authentic approach to creating rapport with audiences seems like the surefire ethical solution for attracting positive exposure. However, many companies struggle to find their natural voice in the cluttered social crowd. In this chapter I'll cover a number of techniques or processes that will help you develop your own 'natural' business voice:

- Develop strategies to represent and promote the interests and requirements of the relationship.

- Use appropriate presentation skills to communicate the goals and objectives of the relationship.

- Effectively communicate the issues, policies and practices of the relationship to a range of audiences, in writing and verbally.

- Obtain feedback to identify and develop ways to improve promotional activities within the available opportunities.

Developing strategies to represent and promote business relationships

It is critical to maintain interest in your contacts and to continually promote ways in which they will benefit from an association with your organisation. The strategies you choose will have to match the audience you are trying to appeal to and the message you are trying to convey to them.

Promoting your organisation's image and reputation online

Whenever you communicate with customers, suppliers or other business contacts, they see you as a representative of the organisation where you work. The image you convey is the one they take away with them as their impression of the organisation, whether it is an accurate representation or not. All of these situations are also opportunities for you to promote your organisation's activities, collective knowledge, staff expertise, culture, contracts, networks, and product and services so the contact can identify the benefits to be gains by maintaining the relationship. Social media/networking promotional strategies include:

- News updates (industry, internal)

- Written reports (eBooks)

- Oral presentations (video)

- Advertisements (banner ads, PPC)

- Representing your organisation at key industry events on- or offline

- Developing and displaying a consistent, professional corporate image

- Arranging meetings with key people

Creating Productive Social Media Relationships

Here are five basic concepts which will establish productive and rewarding social media networks:

1. **Listen to your audience:** Before beginning your contribution to social media communities, take a step back and look at how your company and industry is perceived. Understanding your consumers' needs and wants is the first step to providing them with useful content and support – and adapting to their language is key to developing your strategy. Knowing what kind of content is important to your audience is absolutely essential. The last thing a social media campaign wants to do is to flood communities with an irrelevant, one-directional message. In fact, you will be thrown into the lion's pit, creating new negative impressions and perpetuating existing ones.

2. **Participate in the dialogue:** Become an active member in all discussions, not only topics that will directly relate to sales or conversion. Showing your interest in all areas will instil your values, trust, and opinions across the board. An on-going presence will keep you in the forefront of users' minds as a valuable resource. Your agenda for social networking (hopefully) is not totally self-serving, so try not to come across that way by only putting in your two cents when it's self-promotional.

3. **You don't have to be an expert:** remember, marketing (in more areas than just social media) is subjective and is an on-going learning process. Not always having an answer isn't necessarily a bad thing. As a matter of fact, not having an answer will give your posts a human quality. Individuals, rather than corporations, are going to make a stronger connection in these communities. It is important to develop your message not in industry terms,

50

but in laymen's; we've all heard corporate speak and wondered who these drones are really trying to reach.

4. **Create fresh content:** Some may tag original, fresh content as the most important aspect of being productive with social media. Whether the clichéd phrase "Content is King" is true or not, fresh content does create a community around relevant information and establishes credibility.

5. **Be authentic:** If a social media campaign isn't genuine, authentic, or natural, prepare for an onslaught of negative feedback. Being transparent about your identity and the nature of your message will enhance all other online marketing tactics by showing your consumers the respect they deserve. Deceptive practices may be tempting, and may even show quick results, but it will hinder any opportunity to create a relationship with users. Social media analyst and consultant Jeremiah Owyang has compiled a list of companies and individuals that tried to take shortcuts with social media only to see their efforts backfire. The last thing you want for your campaign is to expend resources and time only to see yourself added to this list.

Tips for running a successful competition on social networks

Competitions are a great way to promote your product or service, but no matter what you want to promote, consider the following tips to help your competition succeed:

- Decide up front what the purpose of your competition is – traffic, likes, following, data, brand buzz.

- Make it extremely easy to enter or participate.

- Incorporate social sharing as part of the entry and voting process.

- Place the competition directly within Facebook or your own website depending on your goals. Remember to adhere to guidelines if using social media sites such as Facebook.

- Follow up with the results and keep the community engaged.

Strategies for creating online business partnerships

To capture the imagination of potential partners you need to come to the table with a very specific and attractive idea. So, what is "attractive" in this context? As in any sales environment, you first need to capture your potential partner's interest by clearly spelling out what is in it for them, using one of the following strategies:

- Suggest introducing them to one or two key people you know could help them.

- Come to the table with a killer eBook that you would allow them to co-brand.

- Ask to interview them for a segment on your podcast.

- Offer to promote their product or service to your online community.

- Create a special offering, gift certificate or sample product and allow them to gift it to their clients.

- Offer to provide some product or service free of charge to them.

- Ask them to teach you the best way to refer them to your clients.

Notice the common thread running through most of the above suggestions – one of the most powerful ways to be more attractive is to give before you get.

Once you've established trust through this initial, genuine purpose, you'll find that the doors to "working together" may naturally swing open, but even if they do not, you'll have established a much more potent method of building relationships in a way that will produce the best kinds of opportunities – those that are mutually beneficial.

Using Presentation Skills To Communicate Your Goals And Objectives For The Relationship

Presenting information professionally takes practice. You can develop a range of skills to ensure you present information so your networks clearly understand the goals and objectives of the relationship between them and your organisation.

Effective verbal communication

Verbal communication is the ability to explain and present your ideas in clear language, to diverse audiences. This includes the ability to tailor your delivery to a given audience, using appropriate styles and approaches, and an understanding of the importance of non-verbal cues in oral communication. Non-verbal communication is the ability to enhance the expression of ideas and concepts without the use of coherent labels, through the use of body language, gestures, facial expression and tone of voice, and also the use of pictures, icons and symbols. Non-verbal communication requires background skills such as the context the message is received, branding and audience awareness.

A large part of the communication used to establish and maintain business networks is done verbally. The ability to communicate, and communicate well, is one of the biggest factors in business success. You could be an excellent designer, but if you're unable to promote your services and communicate effectively with clients and colleagues, your potential is limited. The principal areas where communication is essential include:

- Pitching potential clients

- Client meetings

- Customer service

- Face-to-face networking

- Marketing your business

But we also need to be aware of how we talk to colleagues, chat to contacts, ask customers questions, negotiate in teams, listen to presentations and hold telephone conversations. Put simply, every interaction is a network interaction and whether it's face-to-fact or via some form of social media, you need to be aware of how you are communicating.

Being an effective verbal communicator is the difference between being good and great at what you do. If your business skills are on a par with your competition's, then strong communication skills can put you ahead. Strengthening your communication skills is worth the time and effort, and you may be surprised by how much you benefit from more polished and professional interaction.

Written communication

Written communication is the ability to write effectively in a range of contexts and for a variety of different audiences and purposes. This includes the ability to tailor your writing to a given audience, using appropriate styles and approaches. Different situations will require different types of written materials. Written communication includes:

- Brochures

- Websites

- Advertising

- Letters

It also encompasses electronic communication such as SMS, email, discussion boards, chat rooms and instant messaging,

Written communications are often more formal than verbal communications but in a similar fashion, written communication should be structured to meet the objectives of the presentation and the needs of the target audience.

To communicate the goals and objectives of the relationship you wish to develop with your social network contacts, your written material must stand out from all the other information people receive. You need to first grab people's attention, then gain their interest, create a desire, and then prompt them to act on that desire.

Get to the point quickly. People lose interest easily. You have to make your point clear, concise and include a call to action. People often scan information looking for the highlights. If they don't find the key issues summarised early on, they will become confused and probably lose interest. Keep people interested by combining text and graphics. People can then learn about what you are trying to say in different ways.

As with any communication, it is vital to know your audience. Authors usually know more about their subject than the intended audience, so it is easy to forget that others are not as knowledgeable as you. Follow these three golden rules for written communication:

1. Define your terms.

2. Avoid slang, jargon and unnecessarily technical language.

3. Write clear, plain English.

A final but essential point for written communication in a social media context is that you must ensure you make it easy for people to respond and share your written information.

Barriers to effective communication

Even if we try to simplify our communication processes, barriers come up that can sabotage the message and render it ineffective by the time it gets to those who must act on it. Although there are many barriers that inhibit effective communication, they generally fall into four main categories:

1. Technical

2. Cultural

3. Language

4. Psychological

Technical Barriers

The most common barriers that are likely to occur when using technology to communicate are:

- Availability of financial and other resources required for this purpose.

- The relationship may be affected negatively, unless proper attention is given.

- Implementation of the technology. This will include among other things, developing positive attitude of businesses toward new systems and their training in using the technology effectively.

Cultural Barriers

Each culture has its own rules of communication. Usually, cross-cultural gaffes stem from misjudging situations that involve mingling and communicating with others. These include: the dress code for appointments, the manner in which we introduce ourselves and greet others, expressing thanks to the hosts as well as proper etiquette for the presentation of gifts. While the majority of Australians consider such events to be very routine, the fact remains that the interpretation of these social commitments varies from country to country. If we fail to educate ourselves in advance as to what is and what isn't acceptable, then we prime ourselves for unintentional embarrassment, possibly at the worst given moment. Above all, consider the cultural makeup of the intended audience, seek to understand where there are differences, and fashion the message to ensure that it says what you mean while taking those differences into account.

Language Barriers

Variance in expression or colloquialism is common even among those who speak the same language. The easiest ways to avoid misunderstandings caused by language choice is to minimise the use of slang and idioms, keep your language simple and as free as possible from business speak or (dare I say it?) sports metaphors, and finally, resist the temptation to show off your linguistic ability.

Psychological Barriers (Biases and Assumptions)

Biases

We all have them. A bias is, after all, shaped by our experiences and who we are. However, it becomes an obstacle to effective communication when we consciously or subconsciously choose to speak only to those who are more likely to understand and agree with us. It's natural. But in building relationships and networks, it is also important to extend the reach of our message to those whose biases do not necessarily align with our own.

The workplace, for example, now employs several generations of people. Each generation has its view of the world. Each generation also has its challenges. And yet, the messages you send must find a ways to reach and engage everyone to be effective.

Always acknowledge your own biases first; then look through the lens of those who are least likely to align with your views and listen to what those people are saying; then fashion your message to include something that they can relate to.

Assumptions

It may have been Oscar Wilde who said, *"When you assume, you make an ass out of U and Me"*. Assumptions sabotage effective communication and have the potential to lead everyone down unintended paths. For instance, you may assume that because people are nodding while you speak, they understand and agree with what you are saying. Similarly, if you invite questions about your message and get none, it would be easy to assume there are none. The truth is, few people will risk the potential embarrassment of being the only one who doesn't agree with or understand your message or doesn't know what to ask. To assume they do would be a mistake.

Instead of falling victim to your own assumptions, work on the basis that all your assumptions could be false. Try making your assumptions known to others to determine their validity. Anticipate questions and concerns that could come out of your message and bring them up to encourage conversation.

Communication barriers are always going to be with us because humans are complex beings. I think that's what makes it a challenge…and sometimes a great source of fun.

Effectively Communicate the Issues and Policies Around Social Media Relationships

An office worker was fired after her employer discovered her sex blog. A waitress was fired for venting about a customer on Facebook. A woman lost a job offer at Cisco because of something she said on Twitter. Social media exposes business to significant risks including serious damage to a company's reputation. With a proactive approach you can influence and counteract how your organisation is portrayed on social media.

These incidents illustrate why it might be wise to create a social media policy for your business and your employees.

A good social media policy outlines for employees the corporate guidelines or principles of communicating in the online world. Your social media policy could be your first line of defence to mitigate risk for both employer and employee. You may already have a confidentiality agreement but it might not be enough. Adding a few lines in the employee handbook to clarify that the confidentiality agreement covers employee interactions on social media sites might suffice. But it is usually advisable to create a separate social media policy so as to have something specific on file and accessible to employees so that they are aware of the policy's existence.

There are two approaches to creating a social media policy. You can write a single and complete policy that attempts to address all currently available social media. Or you can write policies as you need them. For example, if your company doesn't have a social media presence on YouTube you may not need to address video usage. But as your business expands, you add a YouTube policy later.

A good social media policy clearly outlines:

- What the company will and will not do online

- What employees can and cannot do online

- What members of the public can and cannot do on company social media accounts

This protects the business by setting boundaries around what is acceptable and what is unacceptable. It also empowers users by letting them know what the limits are, so they can participate without fear of repercussion.

Best practice checklist for writing your social media policy

A good social media policy should be implemented as a living document that will continually change according to your business needs and the evolving nature of the social media environment. The following tips will help you craft a fit for purpose social media policy:

- Discuss the draft policy with all stakeholders involved in social media: marketing, communications, legal, HR, sales, customer service, as well as external etc.

- The policy should support existing company policies and not supersede them.

- It should be customised to fit your organisation's specific needs and operations.

- Make it clear what the policy applies to; e.g. multimedia, social networking websites, blogs and wikis for both professional and personal use.

- Internet postings should not disclose any information that is confidential or proprietary to the company or to any third party that has disclosed information to the company.

- Clarify that if an employee comments on any aspect of the company's business they must clearly identify themselves as an employee and include a disclaimer. Provide a wording for the disclaimer such as, "The views expressed are mine alone and do not necessarily reflect the views of (company name)."

- Personal Internet postings should not include company logos or trademarks unless permission is asked for and granted.

- Personal and business Internet postings must respect copyright, privacy, fair use, financial disclosure, and other applicable laws.

- Your social media policy should include statements about the appropriate ways to interact with the social media community in line with your overall brand identity. It should be available online.

- Give employees the choice to participate in social media (the more the merrier!) but be very clear on the distinction between corporate and personal participation. In other words, encourage employees to be involved in the proper context. Define guiding principles of engagement, to learn or contribute.

The following key issues should also be addressed by your social media policy...

Defining the Rules Of Engagement

Request employees to:

- Be transparent and judicious

- Identify yourself and your role, be honest

- Don't violate privacy or confidentiality policies

- Contribute within your area of expertise

- Be responsible for the content you provide

- Add value to the conversation

- Be a thought leader and be thought-provoking

- It's a conversation, so encourage comments

Disclosure Of Identity

In any networking contact, clarity of identity and personal or business interests (if any) is vital to keeping the relationship open and honest. Below is a sample disclosure of identity policy statement. These points can be included as part of your social media policy.

When communicating with blogs or bloggers on behalf of my company or on topics related to the business of my company, I will:

- *Disclose who I am, who I work for, and any other relevant affiliations from the very first encounter.*

- *Disclose any business/client relationship if I am communicating on behalf of a third party.*

- *Provide a means of communicating with me.*

- *Comply with all laws and regulations regarding disclosure of identity.*

- *I will inform employees, agencies, and advocates that we have a formal relationship of these disclosure policies and take action quickly to correct problems where possible.*

Personal use of social media

The likelihood is that most of your employees will maintain either social media presence or even a personal blog. The below list outlines the best practices for employees who may comment on company-related issues in a personal context.

- If employees write anything related to the business of their employer on personal pages, posts, and comments, they will clearly identify their business affiliation.

- The manner of disclosure can be flexible as long as it is clear to the average reader, directly connected to the relevant post, or provides a means of communicating further (Example disclosure methods could include: usernames that include the company name, link to bio or about me page, or statement in the post itself "I work for __<company>___ and this is my personal opinion.")

- Employees will specifically clarify which posts/comments are their own opinions vs. official corporate statements.

- Writing which does not mention work-related topics does not need to mention the employment relationship.

- If employees blog anonymously they should not discuss matters related to the business of their employer. If employer-related topics are mentioned, they should disclose their affiliation with the company.

Community relations

Part of the beauty of social media use in business is the speed and reach of the communication, including the ability to engage directly and personally with individuals. The following template wording constitutes best practice for businesses interacting with external blogs and bloggers.

When communicating with blogs or bloggers on behalf of my company, I will:

- *Disclose who I am, who I work for and any other relevant affiliations from the very first encounter.*

- *Proactively ask bloggers to be transparent about their relationship and communications with me.*

- *Always be truthful.*

- *Never ask someone else to deceive bloggers for me.*

- *Never ask bloggers to write a fake endorsement or something they do not believe.*

- *Never use off-topic comment for self-promotional intent.*

- *Never take action contrary to the specific boundaries, terms and conditions, and community guidelines set by each blog.*

- *Not use services or technologies for mass-posting comments.*

- *Use extreme care when communicating with minors or blogs intended to be read by minors.*

- *Comply with all laws and regulations regarding disclosure of identity.*

- *Make it clear to your employees and agencies that these rules apply to them.*

Compensation and incentives

Part of your social media policy should look outward, i.e. address the interaction with your wider online community. One common such interaction is the provision of compensation such as rewards, incentives, promotional items, gifts, samples, or review items. This kind of activity should be completely transparent and the guiding policy principles are:

- Review products can be returned at their own discretion.

- Review products must be returned or paid for at fair market value.

- Items of nominal value (low cost product samples or consumables) may be kept.

- Review products should be returned, paid for, or retained by the blogger based on standards for the specific industry. (Examples: restaurant reviewers pay for the meal, tech reviewers return the product, hotels provide complimentary stays.)

- Communicating these policies clearly to the blogger in advance, and asking that they do the same in any post that may result.

- Encouraging bloggers to disclose the source of any compensation directly in any post they write about us.

- If you choose to use paid posts or reviews: ensuring that it is clearly disclosed in the specific post that it is an advertisement.

- Not manipulating advertising, link-trading, or affiliate programs to impact blogger income or traffic.

- Understanding that if you send bloggers products for review, they are not obligated to comment on them at all, and they are free to write a positive, negative or neutral comment.

Agency and contractor disclosure

Of course, it's not only employees who interact on your behalf online, you may have dealings with vendors, agencies, and subcontractors all of whom represent your company in some way. The following wording is a good starting point:

When using external agencies or personnel to communicate on our behalf, I will:

- *Require my agency to disclose its relationship with my company when it conducts blogger relations.*

- *Require my agency to be truthful and never knowingly deceive bloggers.*

- *Publicly acknowledge when my agency and/or related parties act contrary to these policies, and quickly take corrective action where possible.*

- *Require agencies and agency personnel to meet or exceed our internal disclosure requirements.*

- *Require agencies to enforce these requirements on their subcontractors.*

Always discuss and secure formal agreement on these practices before entering into a business relationship with an agency involved in social media.

Consequences

As in any policy, there should be a clear statement detailing the consequences of breaching your social media policy, including the possibility of termination.

Examples And Further Tips For Your Social Media Policy

- **IBM Social Computing Guidelines -**

  http://www.ibm.com/blogs/zz/en/guidelines.html

- **10 Must-Haves for Your Social Media Policy -**

  http://mashable.com/2009/06/02/social-media-policy-musts/

- **Social Media Governance - Policy Database –**

  A listing of social media policies. Referenced by the world's largest brands and agencies - http://socialmediagovernance.com/policies.php

Obtaining feedback to improve promotional activities

As with anything you do in establishing business networks, whether it is expanding your circle of contacts or fine-tuning your listening skills, you should aim for continual improvement. An excellent way to improve your skills in a targeted way is to seek feedback from others, namely those in your social media networks.

How you deal with customer feedback – good and bad – is critical to your brand. But with over 62 percent of consumers turning to social media to tackle their customer service issues, you better have an escalation plan. You don't want a few frustrated customers to go viral with an "Occupy your brand" movement on Twitter.

Sadly, for many customers, logging a complaint on social media channels largely falls on a deaf and comfortably numb ear. Recent studies found that only 35 percent of big retailers respond to customer complaints on Facebook and Twitter. That's quite dismal when you consider what's at stake: profits and PR. Turning frustrated customers into happy campers pays. According to American Express, people who experience great customer service on social media will not only tell 3 times more people, they'll spend 21 percent more, too!

The feedback you collect can be helpful in directing your future social networking activities more effectively. Constructive feedback will be negative as well as positive. Use the feedback to highlight problem areas that require improvement, confirm that you are doing certain things well or poorly, and suggest new areas to explore.

Take time to review how well you are developing and maintaining your business relationships. It is important to stop, take stock, put things into perspective and evaluate how you are going. It is always easier to do things the same way – the way you know. However, there is always room for improvement and seeking feedback is an effective step towards improving your skills.

Feedback can be sought for a number of reasons; for example, to:

- Make sure that the information you have prepared or shared is accurate and sufficient.

- Ensure that the activity you are undertaking is beneficial to your organisation.

- Gauge the impact of the message you are trying to send.

- Evaluate and compare the effectiveness of different media for your purpose.

- Initiate contact with other networks.

- Confirm your target audience is appropriate for your objectives.

- Evaluate the reaction of competitors.

Sources of feedback

Sources of feedback can be internal or external to the organisation. The people you work closely with can be excellent sources of information. Sometimes friends and family can also offer advice. Feedback can also be sought from those you are trying to develop relationships with, including customers, colleagues, contacts, competitors, individuals, and organisations.

Types of feedback

Feedback can be formal or informal. Formal feedback could include:

- An evaluation of your performance.

- Customer satisfaction questionnaires.

- Written complaints.

- Written acknowledgment or work well done.

- Reports; for example, from an advertising agency regarding coverage, sales, and/or market research.

Whereas informal feedback could include:

- Conversations with managers or other colleagues.

- Conversations with network contacts.

- Second-hand reports; for example, about a competitor's activities.

- Audience reaction.

- Organisational visibility; for example, invitations to functions, invitations to speak, media coverage.

- Increase in offers to work collaboratively.

- Increase or decrease in problems occurring; for example, complaints or returned goods.

Analysing feedback

Determining the source and type of feedback you are after really depends on what you want to understand or improve. For example, if you want feedback on the way you present yourself to colleagues, you may want to adopt an informal face-to-face approach, asking a few simple questions. On the other hand, if you are after feedback on ways to improve promotional activities, you may wish to adopt a more formal interview or survey-based approach, including questions on the following areas:

- **Accuracy and sufficiency of information** - Did you give enough information for people to understand your message? Was there anything else you could have included? Was the information accurate? Did people have any other questions that needed to be answered? Was there anything that you missed?

- **Benefits to the organisation** - Did people understand how the organisation

64

would benefit? Was this clearly articulated? Do they agree with these benefits? Are there any benefits (or downsides) that you didn't consider? Were these well-presented?

- **Impact of message** - How did people feel about what you were saying? Do they agree with it? Was the message clearly articulated? What reflections do they have on the way you delivered the message? How could you have increased the impact of your message? What do they intend to do with the information?

- **Use of media** - Did the media used help or hinder? Was it appropriate? Was it used and operated confidently and seamlessly? Would another medium have been more appropriate?

- **Liaison with networks** - Did you liaise appropriately with networks? Should there have been more/less liaison? Are there any suggestions or input from network members that should have been incorporated? Did all appropriate network members receive the message? Do you have a strong relationship with network members? How can this be improved?

- **Appropriateness of audience** - Were the right people hearing your message? Was anybody missing? Were there people who didn't need to be there? Was the message delivered in a way that was appropriate for the audience?

- **Participation of competitors** - Did competitors participate? What was the response? Was the message appropriate for competitors to hear? Was any commercially-sensitive information discussed?

END OF CHAPTER ACTIVITY – Examples of Outstanding Social Networking

What examples of social networking activity from businesses have captured your attention recently? What was it about them that made them stand out? How did they communicate the relationship the organisation had to offer?

Conclusion

This book has been a passion of mine. The idea is to help other businesses learn from my media and communication experience. What I hope comes through is that in itself, social media isn't so much a new activity as a new (and exciting and ever-evolving) set of tools to carry out a long-standing marketing activity: networking to build your business. But while the goals – leads, sales, profit – may be the same, you do need to understand the rules of this new online arena that offers so much. In this ever evolving, expanding and enduring communication channel there is an undeniable necessity to be digitally literate. As social human beings, we now need to continually educate ourselves on the most effective ways to utilise new technology to achieve not only our business objectives but our personal and social ones as well.

In business, strategy is everything - you must plan carefully how to use social media to your best advantage. Know what you're aiming to achieve and know your target market. Choose the right social media channels to achieve your marketing goals. Ensure you seek out and work with the right people. You're looking to create value, engage meaningfully, build credibility and above all, collaborate – never forget that communication in the social media environment is both rapid and 360 degrees. And as you go, measure your progress and results carefully and adjust and refine your approach.

Be aware of the pitfalls too. In social media, reputations can be lost overnight. You need to understand your brand and have a social media policy that will protect with guidelines on professional and balanced (and calm!) online interactions.

All information in this book has come from working in various industries implementing digital marketing strategies and one thing I can guarantee is that when it comes to social media, one size doesn't fit all. There are no short cuts and no magic pills.

Think of it like going to the gym, if you exercise once or twice a week you will see only small changes over a long period of time. Compare that to changing your whole lifestyle and incorporating gym sessions every day with nutrition and wellness. We all know that the second scenario will yield much better results for your body over the first. So consider your business culture and the commitment you are willing to make to build a successful social media presence. Then do it!

Whatever level that commitment is, whatever your strategy involves, I wish you the best of results.

Lisa Harrison

GLOSSARY

Blog - developed from the term **web log**, is a discussion or information site published on the World Wide Web.

Blog can also be used as a verb, meaning to maintain or add content to a blog.

Content marketing - a form of marketing that involves the sharing of information (i.e. content) in order to attract potential customers or clients.

eBooks - downloadable electronic books.

Network base - within social media terms a network base is defined as the people whom you are connected with on your social networking accounts.

ROI – Short for "return on investment", ROI can refer to any measures or metrics used to establish the value gained from a purchase or improvement; put simply, it's about determining whether the results of an initiative were worth the time and money invested in it.

RSS - An RSS file contains details of the latest items available within a website, it helps you keep up to date without having to check the site itself.

SEO - Short for "search engine optimisation", SEO is the process of increasing the amount of visitors to a website by obtaining a high-ranking placement in the search results page of a search engine. The higher a website ranks in the results of a search, the greater the chance the site will be visited by a user.

SMM - Social Media Manager: an individual that handles the company's social media marketing strategy needs.

Web 2.0 - Web 2.0 does not refer to a particular technology but to a general trend. It is considered to incorporate user-generated content, collaboration, online networking and social media, and personalisation within the digital realm. It is the ability for users to add and edit content - contributing online using different types of technology and interactive media, and creating more personalised web experiences.

Web 3.0 – Web 3.0 indicates the capability of a more sophisticated interaction between users and websites in which, for example, the technology will analyse and 'understand' more detailed queries and provide tailored and more accurate answers.

Web 4.0 – Web 4.0 is a similar level of interaction to Web 3.0 (approaching the appearance at least of artificial intelligence) but combined seamlessly with mobile technology.

Webinar - web conferencing used to conduct seminars, demos, training or live meetings.

www.ingramcontent.com/pod-product-compliance
Lightning Source LLC
Chambersburg PA
CBHW071306170526
45165CB00003B/1444